INSIDE THE WORLD OF THE HAVES AND THE HAVE YACHTS

A Reflective Journey Inspired by The Haves and the Have Yachts

By

Richard Wills

Chapter 1: The New Gilded Age

Section 1: Wealth Without Limits

The phrase "too much wealth" used to sound like a contradiction in terms. In America's cultural and economic ethos, more has always meant better. But in *The Haves and the Have Yachts*, Evan Osnos pulls back the velvet curtain on the ultra-rich, exposing a class so wealthy it has not only transcended middle-class dreams but also broken free from collective accountability. Their lives are not just abundant—they are unrecognizably extravagant.

Osnos introduces us to billionaires whose yachts cost $400 million, not as rare indulgences but as required accessories in elite circles. These aren't yachts—

7

they're floating cities, armed with anti-paparazzi drones and submarine garages. Helicopters are a basic amenity. These symbols are not merely signs of wealth; they are declarations of detachment, monuments to what happens when wealth becomes unlimited and unchecked.

Reflection Prompt 1: What Is "Too Much"?

In your view, where should we draw the line between wealth and excess?

What does "enough" mean to you personally?

Have you ever felt the discomfort of witnessing extreme wealth? What triggered it?

The Psychological Toll of Unlimited Wealth

Osnos shows that wealth without limits doesn't create safety—it creates paranoia. Billionaires build bunkers, not just mansions. They fear uprising, exposure, theft, irrelevance. Behind the scenes, financial excess morphs into emotional distress. They worry about being "outyachted," about their children losing ambition, about being robbed by the very society that enriched them.

And yet, they continue to accumulate—not for survival, but for status. In this world, being wealthy isn't about having money; it's about being wealthier than someone else.

Exercise: Wealth Thermometer

Use the scale below to mark where you believe wealth becomes problematic:

- $1 million

- $10 million
- $100 million
- $500 million
- $1 billion
- $10 billion

Then answer: Why does that point feel like a moral boundary for you?

The Disconnection of Mega-Wealth

As Osnos portrays, the ultra-rich live in a dimension of their own—airports, clinics, schools, even climates are optional to them. They can pay to avoid every inconvenience and interaction. But in doing so, they lose something essential: shared human experience.

"Wealth beyond a certain point doesn't just separate people—it isolates them."

Reflection Prompt 2: Who Are the "Untouchables" in Your World?

Think about people in your society you never directly interact with.

Are they the ultra-wealthy? Are they the ultra-poor? Why are those interactions missing?

What systems support that separation?

Section 2: Historical Echoes

The Gilded Age of the late 19th century was named for a reason: gold on the surface, rot underneath. Titans like Rockefeller, Vanderbilt, and Carnegie amassed fortunes that dwarfed those of kings, all while workers died in unsafe factories and children labored in mines. Today, we are living in what many call the "Second Gilded Age."

Osnos doesn't make this comparison lightly. He shows how today's elite deploy the same strategies as the old barons:

- **Philanthropy as Public Relations**
- **Influence-peddling in politics**
- **Industrial dominance through monopolies**
- **Inheritance as aristocracy**

Where 19th-century moguls built railroads, steel empires, and oil trusts, today's oligarchs dominate data, media, and private equity. They aren't just creating wealth—they're shaping reality.

Case Study: From Carnegie Libraries to Tech Billionaire Spaceships

Andrew Carnegie built thousands of public libraries as a nod to civic duty. Today, billionaires like Jeff Bezos and Elon Musk race to colonize Mars—not to expand access to knowledge or opportunity, but to escape the planet they helped degrade.

Reflection Prompt 3: Who Are Today's Carnegies?

Think of a modern billionaire who invests heavily in public good.

What motivates them: duty, guilt, legacy, ego, or something else?

How do their actions compare to their rhetoric?

Repeating the Pattern

History doesn't repeat itself, but it often rhymes. The same concentration of wealth, political manipulation, and public backlash seen in the first Gilded Age are all alive today—just digitized and globalized.

The original Gilded Age sparked the Progressive Era: trust-busting, labor laws, income tax. What will this era spark?

Journal Prompt: What Comes After the Gilding?

If this is the Second Gilded Age, what is the next chapter we must write as a society?

What reforms, awakenings, or reckonings do you believe are coming—or should come?

Section 3: Mapping the Class Divide

We live in a world where someone can drop $30 million on a painting while another person sleeps on cardboard two blocks away. Wealth inequality isn't just a statistic—it's a street scene, a neighborhood line, a lunchroom barrier.

Osnos compels us to confront not just national disparities but personal ones. He makes class visceral: the security guards watching the yacht party they'll never attend, the landscapers trimming hedges of homes they'll never afford.

Visible and Invisible Class Lines

Some class lines are easy to see:

- Private jets vs. economy seats
- Designer clothes vs. dollar store uniforms
- Exclusive schools vs. public districts

Others are more subtle:

- Vocabulary and accents
- Access to legal help
- Expectations of health and longevity

Exercise: Class Inventory

List the ways class appears in your day:

- Where you shop
- How you commute
- Who does your service work
- What insurance coverage you have

Then ask: What does this reveal about your position—and your blind spots?

The Myth of the Middle Class

Most Americans self-identify as middle class—even millionaires. Why? Because admitting you're rich implies guilt. And admitting you're poor implies failure. So we cling to "middle" like a life raft.

Osnos dismantles this myth by showing how wealth stratification is sharper than ever. In reality, the middle class is shrinking. There's a canyon between surviving and thriving.

Journal Prompt: Where Do You Belong—And Why?

Do you consider yourself working, middle, upper, or wealthy class?

What shaped that identity: income, upbringing, community, education?

Has that identity shifted over time?

Bridging the Divide

Knowing where we stand in the class system is the first step. The next is asking: What role do we want to play in bridging it? It doesn't require guilt—but it does demand awareness, curiosity, and courage.

Reflection Prompt 4: The Bridge-Building Blueprint

What's one step you can take to increase class awareness in your world?

Examples: mentoring, diversifying your network, paying fair wages, reading class-conscious books, funding systemic change.

✍ Wrap-Up Exercise: Gilded Mirror

Look in the Mirror—Not for Shame, but for Clarity.

Answer these final prompts to reflect on your own place in the New Gilded Age:

1. How do you benefit from the current economic system?
2. How might your life be different if you were born two income tiers lower?
3. What emotions arise when you see extreme wealth: envy, admiration, anger, indifference? What do those emotions teach you?
4. What kind of world do you want to help build—one that protects yachts or one that protects dignity?

✅ Chapter 1 Summary:

- **Wealth Without Limits** has become not just a reality but a social experiment in isolation, insecurity, and symbolism.
- **Historical Echoes** show that today's billionaires are the heirs of past barons, repeating cycles of accumulation and control.
- **Mapping the Class Divide** reminds us that inequality isn't abstract—it's personal, visible, and reversible, if we choose awareness and action.

Chapter 2: The Yacht as Metaphor

Section 1: What Luxury Reveals

The superyacht is not just a boat. It is a floating fortress of status, secrecy, and insulation. In *The Haves and the Have Yachts*, Evan Osnos uses the yacht as a masterful metaphor—one that sails smoothly through the waters of wealth but anchors deeply in the psychology and symbolism of the ultra-rich.

At first glance, luxury is just a display of taste or reward for hard work. But look closer, and it reveals something else: a narrative of power, control, and cultural distance. The scale of wealth revealed by superyachts (some longer than football fields and costlier than small nations) tells us that luxury isn't about need—it's about *signaling*.

Luxury as Identity Statement

Ultra-luxury doesn't merely serve a purpose—it *proclaims* one. Whether it's a gold-plated faucet or a climate-controlled wine cellar below deck, every detail says, "I can." Not "I need," not "I value," not "I enjoy"—but "I can."

This is what sociologist Thorstein Veblen called *conspicuous consumption*—spending designed to show off status. The yacht, in this light, becomes the ultimate badge of elite identity. It is the reward, the shield, and the billboard, all in one.

Reflection Prompt 1: What Do You Want People to Know About You—Without Saying a Word?

Think of the items you own or the services you use that reflect your identity.

Do you buy for utility, status, expression, or comfort?

What do your choices reveal to others?

The Yacht as a Power Signal

Yachts are not just displays of wealth; they're tools of influence. The ability to invite politicians, celebrities, or CEOs aboard a private floating world grants billionaires a kind of gravitational pull. These spaces aren't just leisure—they're leverage.

Osnos describes how, on these vessels, deals are made in swim trunks and billion-dollar trust plans are finalized over champagne. The privacy afforded by yachts makes them zones of unregulated power, removed from oversight and accountability.

Exercise: Map the Power Signals

Draw a diagram of power and influence tools you've seen or used (examples might include professional networks, alumni associations, luxury brands, gated communities, etc.).

Now label whether each tool includes **visibility**, **exclusivity**, or **control**.

Section 2: Symbols of Separation

Luxury, in its highest form, doesn't just add comfort—it creates distance. The design and function of superyachts illustrate how wealth is increasingly used to isolate rather than integrate. Through architecture, technology, and location, the rich are building worlds-within-worlds—entirely separated from the rest of society.

Designing for Detachment

Osnos details how yachts are outfitted not just with comfort but with privacy. Facial recognition security, noise-masking systems, hidden escape routes. Many have zero lines of sight from the outside world. The message is clear: You can look, but you can't see. You can admire, but you can't approach.

Just like private compounds and high-walled estates, yachts are designed to repel. They are aesthetic fortresses—meant to project style while denying access.

Reflection Prompt 2: What Spaces in Your Life Are Designed to Exclude?

Consider places like country clubs, offices, schools, churches, or even your home.

Who do these spaces *welcome*—and who do they *push away*?

Technology as a Barrier

The ultra-wealthy use technology to maintain this distance. Encrypted phones, gated surveillance, private health care apps, AI-powered assistants, climate-controlled travel bubbles. These tools don't just make life easier—they make it *other*.

On a yacht, a billionaire can fly in chefs, stream from servers in Luxembourg, and never experience a local culture despite sailing around the world. The aim is not integration, but insulation.

Exercise: The Tech Divide

Make two lists:

- Tools of *access* (tech that brings people together—e.g., public Wi-Fi, social media, rideshare apps)
- Tools of *exclusion* (tech that creates privilege—e.g., concierge services, encrypted networks, AI gatekeeping)

Now circle which list dominates your daily life.

Geography of Separation

Superyachts symbolize the rich's ability to *opt out*—not just of discomfort, but of democracy. They can escape taxes by docking in Monaco, avoid politics by sailing international waters, or bypass legal scrutiny through flag-hopping registration.

Wealth becomes geographic freedom. Osnos captures this when he writes about billionaires' "liquidity"—not just of money, but of place, responsibility, and allegiance.

"For the ultra-rich, borders are porous, but laws are optional."

Journal Prompt: What Does It Mean to Be 'Rooted'?

Do you consider yourself grounded in your community, country, or values?

How would your life change if you had the option to "sail away" from every inconvenience?

Section 3: Reflection – What's Your "Yacht"?

Not everyone owns a yacht, but most of us build bubbles. We choose neighborhoods where we feel comfortable, we scroll feeds that affirm our beliefs, we use services that cater to our schedules. These choices are not inherently wrong—but they matter.

The "yacht" is a metaphor for whatever we use to separate ourselves from discomfort, difference, or reality. It might be:

- **Social circles** that exclude
- **Digital filters** that narrow your view
- **Financial buffers** that blind you to hardship
- **Education privilege** that distances you from systemic issues

Reflection Prompt 3: Name Your Yacht

What do you use—consciously or unconsciously—to stay in control?

What kinds of people, ideas, or experiences do you keep at a distance?

Why?

Interrogating Privilege Without Shame

Privilege is not a personal flaw. It's an unearned advantage. The key is not to feel guilty—but to become *conscious*. Osnos' work pushes us to recognize that separation becomes dangerous when we stop seeing it.

Your "yacht" may be your university degree, your skin color, your income, your passport. What matters is what you do with it.

Exercise: Privilege Mapping Wheel

Create a circle divided into these segments:

- Wealth
- Race
- Gender
- Education
- Ability
- Nationality
- Language
- Religion
- Citizenship

Color each segment from light (low privilege) to dark (high privilege).

Then ask: Where are you advantaged—and where are you not?

Stepping Off the Yacht

If the yacht is a metaphor for separation, then stepping off is a metaphor for solidarity. It means:

- Visiting neighborhoods you don't usually go to
- Talking to people who challenge your worldview
- Investing time and money in communities unlike your own
- Choosing transparency over privacy, inclusion over comfort

Journal Prompt: How Can You Step Off Your Yacht?

Think of one practical way you can reduce social, economic, or psychological separation this week.

It might involve service, listening, donating, or inviting.

What does it cost you? What might it open?

✅ **Chapter 2 Summary:**

- The yacht is more than a vessel—it's a *value system*, reflecting power, control, and distance.
- Ultra-luxury is not about comfort; it's about *separation*, constructed through design, technology, and geography.

- Everyone has a "yacht"—a set of privileges or buffers that remove them from discomfort. Awareness is the first step toward using that privilege for connection, not isolation.

Chapter 3: Inside the Billionaire Mindset

Section 1: Fear of Falling

When we think of billionaires, we imagine people so insulated from suffering, so secure in their wealth, that they must live in a state of complete peace. But as Evan Osnos reveals, that's far from reality. In fact, many of the world's ultra-rich live in a state of heightened fear—fear of falling, of losing it all, of being unmasked, dethroned, or devoured by the very forces that enriched them.

Beneath the surface of opulence lies a psychological fragility, a gnawing awareness that the system they dominate is inherently unstable—and that their place within it is neither permanent nor protected.

The Anxiety of Affluence

Osnos paints vivid portraits of billionaires who install bunker-level security in their homes, stockpile escape helicopters, and rehearse "bug-out" plans. They are obsessed not just with *holding onto* wealth, but with escaping its consequences—economic collapse, political revolution, or climate catastrophe.

To outsiders, this seems absurd. What do you flee *from* when you have everything? The answer is powerlessness. These billionaires fear being caught without control—over others, over their image, over their environment.

Reflection Prompt 1: What Do You Fear Losing?

Think about the aspects of your life you most strive to protect—reputation, comfort, income, stability.

Are those fears rooted in experience, or in imagination?

How do those fears shape your decisions?

Precarity at the Top

What's often misunderstood is that hyper-wealth doesn't eliminate insecurity—it magnifies it. A billionaire might not fear hunger, but they might fear irrelevance. They might not fear eviction, but they fear being surpassed by a rival. Their stakes are social, symbolic, and strategic.

Osnos writes about the *social arms race*—how billionaires constantly upgrade their possessions, lifestyles, and networks to remain competitive. Yachts get longer, homes get smarter, parties get more exclusive. This isn't just about indulgence—it's about *status survival*.

Exercise: Your Status Metrics

List 3-5 things that give you a sense of security or identity (e.g., job title, income level, number of followers, education, relationships).

Now ask: If one were taken away, how would that affect your sense of worth?

The Illusion of Control

At its core, much of billionaire behavior centers on controlling uncertainty. Through private medical teams, boutique education for their children, and political lobbying, they attempt to make the unpredictable predictable. But reality, of course, resists.

Pandemics, protests, and populism have reminded even the most powerful that some forces can't be bought or avoided.

"The more wealth one has, the more life becomes about building walls—against threat, against change, against truth."

Journal Prompt: When Have You Tried to Control the Uncontrollable?

Describe a time when money, planning, or privilege couldn't shield you from uncertainty.

What did you learn about yourself or the world in that moment?

Section 2: Ethical Storytelling

How do billionaires *live with themselves* in a world so unevenly structured in their favor? Osnos reveals the narrative tools they use to reconcile—or obscure—their moral dissonance. This is the art of **ethical storytelling**: constructing a personal myth that justifies extraordinary privilege.

The Meritocracy Myth

One of the most common billionaire stories is that of *self-made success*. They portray themselves as underdogs who pulled themselves up by their bootstraps—even when those "boots" included elite education, family loans, and inherited networks.

This myth serves a double purpose:

1. It flatters the individual's ego.
2. It absolves them of responsibility for inequality.

If wealth is the product of merit, then poverty must be the result of laziness or failure. This is how structural inequality becomes personalized—and dismissed.

Reflection Prompt 2: What's the Story You Tell Yourself About Your Success?

Who helped you get where you are? What advantages did you inherit?

Are there parts of your story that feel uncomfortable to admit—but important to acknowledge?

Philanthropy as Moral Offset

Osnos also exposes how many billionaires use philanthropy as a way to cleanse their public image. Lavish donations are announced in press releases, often accompanied by minimal systemic change. These acts of giving are less about justice and more about **moral math**: spend $1 million on charity to justify earning $100 million in tax breaks.

This creates a system where the giver gets *more power* from giving than the recipient does from receiving.

Case Study Prompt: Analyze a Famous Philanthropist

Choose someone like Bill Gates, MacKenzie Scott, or Elon Musk.

What causes do they support? What methods do they use?

Do they challenge or reinforce the system that created their wealth?

Narratives of Benevolent Power

Many billionaires cast themselves as global stewards—those best positioned to solve humanity's problems. They bypass governments and elected leaders, instead trusting their own instincts and tech-driven ideologies.

But as Osnos warns, this is a dangerous delusion. Believing that money grants wisdom—or that wealth equals virtue—can lead to real-world harm.

Exercise: Benevolence or Control?

Think of a recent instance where a wealthy individual or organization stepped in to "help" (e.g., disaster relief, education reform, pandemic response).

Ask: Did they invite collaboration—or command authority? Did they solve problems—or restructure systems in their image?

Section 3: Inheritance, Identity, and Influence

Behind every billionaire is a story about legacy. Some inherit fortunes; others pass them down. Either way, Osnos shows that the obsession with control extends across generations. Wealth is not only a tool for power—it is a language of identity.

The Weight of Legacy

Osnos introduces heirs who feel both burdened and empowered by their family fortunes. Some attempt to do better—founding impact initiatives or ethical funds. Others double down— expanding empires and defending dynasties.

In both cases, inheritance becomes a mirror of values. It's not just money—it's belief systems, ideologies, blind spots.

Reflection Prompt 3: What Have You Inherited—Tangible or Intangible?

Consider money, beliefs, habits, trauma, expectations, reputations.

How do you carry your inheritance—and how do you question it?

Identity Built on Wealth

When your name becomes synonymous with money, it shapes every interaction. Billionaires often struggle to distinguish between genuine relationships and transactional ones. Their identity becomes wrapped in wealth—so much so that they can't imagine life without it.

Osnos describes people whose sense of *self* disintegrates when they face a financial dip—not because they can't afford basics, but because they don't know who they are without affluence.

Journal Prompt: Who Are You Without Your Titles or Income?

Strip away labels like "professional," "provider," or "achiever."

What's left? What anchors your identity beyond external markers?

The Ripple of Influence

Finally, Osnos explores how billionaires influence not just markets but minds. Through media ownership, think tank funding, university donations, and lobbying, they shape public narratives and political outcomes.

This influence often hides behind "philanthropy" or "thought leadership," but its impact is deep and lasting. Billionaires can reshape entire disciplines, redefine public discourse, or even determine election outcomes—often without transparency.

"Billionaire influence is not a loud engine—it's a quiet tide. It moves everything without being seen."

Exercise: Trace the Influence Web

Pick a recent policy, cultural trend, or public controversy. Research whether billionaire money played a role (via funding, media, lobbying, or tech platforms).

What did you discover? Were you surprised?

✅ Chapter 3 Summary:

- **Fear of Falling** drives billionaires to build psychological and physical fortresses, revealing that insecurity doesn't disappear with money—it evolves.
- **Ethical Storytelling** allows the rich to justify their wealth through myths of meritocracy, selective philanthropy, and benevolent control.

- **Inheritance, Identity, and Influence** show that wealth shapes how people see themselves, how they're seen by others, and how they subtly or explicitly mold the world.

✍️ Wrap-Up Reflection: Wealth and the Self

Answer the following to consolidate your insights from this chapter:

1. What's one narrative you've internalized about wealth that you now question?
2. In what ways does your identity depend on economic stability or achievement?
3. What's one way you can decenter wealth in your life—not by rejecting money, but by prioritizing other values?
4. If you had billionaire-level resources, how would you *avoid* the traps described in this chapter?

Chapter 4: How Inequality Warps Democracy

Section 1: The Politics of the Ultra-Rich

Democracy rests on the ideal of *equal voice*. One person, one vote. But Evan Osnos peels back that ideal and reveals a darker reality: in today's political ecosystem, money talks louder than people. Billionaires—armed with limitless financial firepower—can reshape laws, sidestep accountability, and effectively override the public will.

In *The Haves and the Have Yachts*, Osnos doesn't just critique inequality—he shows how it mutates democracy into oligarchy. Through political donations, policy lobbying, and back-channel influence, the ultra-rich don't just play the game of politics—they *own the field.*

Campaign Finance: Legalized Leverage

In the post–Citizens United era, political contributions are speech. And billionaires speak fluently. Osnos outlines how individuals like Sheldon Adelson, Peter Thiel, and the Koch brothers have poured hundreds of millions into Super PACs, think tanks, and media networks. Their goal? To shape agendas that benefit the elite: deregulation, tax loopholes, privatization.

These aren't bribes—they're *investments*. And the return on investment is staggering. A few million spent on lobbying can yield billions in tax breaks.

Reflection Prompt 1: Whose Voice Gets Heard?

Think of a political issue you care about.

How easy would it be for you to meet with a policymaker?

Now imagine you had $1 billion—how would that access change?

Revolving Doors and Quiet Power

Beyond campaign donations, the ultra-rich wield power through the **revolving door**: hiring former politicians, influencing judicial appointments, or placing lobbyists in government advisory roles. Osnos shows how billionaires aren't just bankrolling politics—they're embedded in it.

Think tanks funded by the rich produce white papers. Billionaire-run media outlets shape narratives. Private meetings at luxury retreats set the tone for national policy—often beyond public scrutiny.

Exercise: Follow the Money

Pick a recent law or regulation. Research which lobbyists, donors, or organizations supported or opposed it.

Ask: Was this a people-driven change—or a money-driven one?

The Disguised Nature of Control

What makes billionaire influence so dangerous is how invisible it often is. It hides behind "philanthropy," "thought leadership," or "innovation." These sanitized labels mask the reality: concentrated power is making public decisions without public consent.

"The ultra-wealthy don't need to run for office. They just buy the rules that govern everyone else."

Journal Prompt: Where Have You Seen Power Without Visibility?

Think about organizations, systems, or leaders you've encountered.

Who makes the rules—and how visible are they to the people affected?

Section 2: Regulation Evasion

If democracy is about shared accountability, inequality erodes it from the top. Osnos shows how the rich use wealth not just to gain power—but to *avoid* its consequences. In the eyes of the law, we are *not* all equal.

From offshore accounts to tax shelters, from private arbitration to diplomatic immunity, the billionaire class moves through a different legal universe—one where accountability is optional and punishment is rare.

Tax Avoidance: Legal, But Not Moral

One of the clearest ways inequality distorts democracy is through taxation. Osnos reveals how billionaires pay *less* in effective tax rates than schoolteachers or janitors—not through fraud, but through *strategy*.

They use trusts, charitable foundations, offshore vehicles, and shell corporations to shift wealth around. What's legal for them is often inaccessible to others. It's not just a matter of *evading* tax—it's a matter of *engineering* immunity.

Case Study Prompt: The ProPublica Reports

In 2021, ProPublica released data showing how some of America's wealthiest paid virtually no income tax for years.

- How did they do it?
- What was your reaction?
- Did the exposure change anything?

Private Justice Systems

Another hidden mechanism of inequality is the privatization of justice. Osnos discusses how the wealthy avoid court through **private arbitration**, **non-disclosure agreements**, and elite legal counsel. While average citizens rely on overburdened public courts, the rich write their own rules in boardrooms and yachts.

Even in clear cases of wrongdoing—corporate fraud, sexual harassment, environmental damage—the consequences are often settled quietly, with no admission of guilt and minimal transparency.

Exercise: Two-Tiered Justice

Think of a time when someone with power escaped public accountability.

Now contrast that with a story of someone punished for a minor crime (e.g., petty theft, public protest).

What systems allowed these outcomes?

Geographic and Jurisdictional Escape

Osnos details how the super-rich use geography as a defense mechanism. Need to dodge U.S. taxes? Establish a shell company in the Cayman Islands. Facing legal scrutiny? Relocate to a non-extradition country. Afraid of backlash? Build a floating estate in international waters.

Borders, for billionaires, are flexible. Citizenship is optional. Laws are obstacles to be sidestepped—not systems to be respected.

Reflection Prompt 2: What Would You Do With No Legal Boundaries?

If you knew you couldn't be caught or punished, what would you change about your behavior?

Now ask: Why don't some of the ultra-rich hesitate?

Section 3: Your Voice in the System

Osnos doesn't end in cynicism. Instead, he invites us to examine where democracy *can* be reclaimed—and how regular people can assert agency even in an unequal system. Change won't come from yachts or private jets. It comes from people who choose to engage, organize, and disrupt.

The Myth of Powerlessness

It's easy to feel small in a billionaire-dominated world. But as history shows, mass movements have always been the real engine of democratic change—from the Civil Rights movement to climate activism to labor unions.

Billionaires may fund politics, but they cannot *replace* the people. The myth that "nothing changes" is itself a tool of the elite. Apathy serves those who already have power.

Reflection Prompt 3: Where Have You Seen Collective Action Work?

Think of a protest, campaign, or reform effort that succeeded—local or global.

What made it effective?

What lessons does it offer for today?

The Role of Transparency

One key to restoring democracy is transparency. Exposing who funds what, who influences whom, and how decisions are made. Osnos stresses that investigative journalism, whistleblowers, and public watchdogs are vital to rebalancing the scales.

But transparency must be matched with literacy. We must *learn how systems work* to challenge them.

Exercise: Power Literacy Quiz

Can you answer the following?

1. Who is your local representative?
2. What laws govern campaign donations in your country?
3. How does corporate lobbying operate in your capital?

If you're unsure, that's okay. Use this as a starting point to dig deeper.

Participating With Purpose

Not everyone has money to donate—but everyone has influence to wield. Whether it's voting, volunteering, unionizing, organizing online, or supporting watchdog journalism, democracy thrives on participation.

Osnos reminds us that the billionaire class is powerful—but not omnipotent. Their dominance depends on public disengagement. The more we pay attention, the harder it becomes for them to operate in the shadows.

Journal Prompt: How Do You Show Up as a Citizen?

Are you active in local politics? Do you support transparency initiatives?

How can you use your time, voice, or skills to influence change—even on a small scale?

✅ Chapter 4 Summary:

- **The Politics of the Ultra-Rich** reveal how money now sets the rules in our democracy, reshaping agendas and bypassing public input.
- **Regulation Evasion** shows that billionaires operate within legal frameworks they've largely helped write, escaping the very systems meant to regulate them.
- **Your Voice in the System** highlights that reclaiming democracy depends not on wealth, but on collective awareness, participation, and persistent action.

✍️ Wrap-Up Reflection: Democracy in a Billionaire's World

1. Where have you seen democracy eroded by money?
2. What privileges do you have that allow you to participate in shaping society?
3. What's one issue you care about that you've been silent on?
4. What specific, doable action can you take this month to strengthen democratic fairness— write, vote, volunteer, speak?

Chapter 5: The Hidden Costs of Extreme Wealth

Section 1: Who Pays for the Yacht?

Billionaires do not build their empires in a vacuum. For every extravagant yacht that Osnos describes, there are hundreds—if not thousands—of people whose labor, land, and silence made it possible. Wealth is not just accumulated—it is *extracted*. And the costs, though invisible to the buyer, are painfully real to those who pay them.

In this section, we trace the economic, social, and environmental tolls of extreme wealth. Because luxury has a price—and someone, somewhere, always picks up the tab.

The Human Cost of Production

To build a $600 million yacht requires global networks of shipbuilders, engineers, laborers, and suppliers. But many of these workers earn minimum wage, endure unsafe conditions, and are excluded from the final product they help create.

Osnos captures the stark contrast: waitstaff serving truffle risotto in the sun-drenched dining room, returning at night to windowless bunk beds below deck. These aren't just service jobs—they are symbols of hierarchy.

"The yacht is a microcosm of global inequality—opulence afloat, inequality below sea level."

Reflection Prompt 1: Who Makes Your Comfort Possible?

List 5 services or products you rely on each day (e.g., food delivery, tech devices, clothes).

Can you trace who makes them? What are their working conditions, pay, and protections?

The Outsourcing of Consequences

The rich rarely *see* the full consequences of their consumption. Factory emissions are outsourced to the Global South. Waste is dumped far from private beaches. Resources are extracted from regions where environmental and labor protections are weakest.

This separation allows the ultra-wealthy to enjoy guilt-free consumption, but the damage accumulates elsewhere—in polluted rivers, sickened communities, exploited economies.

Exercise: Global Cost Mapping

Pick one luxury item (e.g., smartphone, leather handbag, cruise experience).

- Where was it made?
- Who produced it?
- What was the environmental toll?

Sketch a "cost map" showing the social and environmental price along the supply chain.

Opportunity Hoarding

Extreme wealth doesn't just deprive through exploitation—it also hoards opportunity. Billionaires secure the best education, real estate, and financial tools, creating closed loops of advantage. When access is monopolized, equity becomes impossible.

Osnos highlights how elite schools, investment funds, and legal loopholes act like velvet ropes—ensuring only the already wealthy can pass through. For everyone else, the ladder is broken.

Journal Prompt: What Ladders Have You Used—Or Been Denied?

Think of moments when an institution opened a door for you—or didn't.

Was that access based on merit, luck, or legacy?

Section 2: The Emotional Toll of Inequality

Beyond economics, inequality imposes deep psychological and emotional costs—on all sides. Osnos does not portray billionaires as villains, but as people trapped in systems of status, anxiety, and moral disconnection. Likewise, those without wealth are affected not just materially, but spiritually.

The Rich and the Restless

Many of the ultra-rich, Osnos writes, are deeply insecure. They fear losing wealth, losing relevance, or losing face among their peers. Living among the 0.01% doesn't inspire peace—it creates competition. There is no "enough," only more.

Isolation, paranoia, and performance anxiety are common. Some hire security teams for their children. Others seek therapists to cope with "legacy pressure." Surrounded by yes-men, many don't know who to trust.

Reflection Prompt 2: What Would You Lose If You Had Everything?

Imagine you had unlimited money.

What aspects of life would improve—and which might degrade (e.g., authenticity, intimacy, creativity)?

The Emotional Cost of Being Left Behind

For those outside the elite, witnessing vast inequality breeds disillusionment, envy, and anger. It erodes the idea of fairness. When effort no longer correlates with reward, motivation plummets. Why work hard if you can't catch up?

Osnos notes how this resentment fuels populism, conspiracy theories, and radical politics—not always in productive directions. The psychological wound of being excluded becomes political fire.

Exercise: Inequality and Emotion

List your emotional responses when you:

- See someone driving a $300,000 car
- Hear about billionaire space tourism
- Struggle to pay bills while corporations announce record profits

Now reflect: What do these emotions teach you?

Class-Based Shame and Silence

Wealth inequality also creates cultural gaps in how we talk—or don't talk—about money. Shame runs deep: the poor are blamed for being poor, and the rich often feel guilty or silent about their wealth.

Osnos shows that many wealthy individuals refuse to discuss their privileges openly. Likewise, people living in poverty are often made invisible—pushed to the margins of both geography and conversation.

Journal Prompt: What's Your Money Story?

Growing up, what messages did you receive about wealth and worth?

Were you encouraged to talk about money—or stay silent?

How does that affect you today?

Section 3: Discomfort as a Compass

Discomfort is not something to avoid—it is something to *notice*. Osnos teaches us that the discomfort we feel around extreme wealth is not dysfunction—it is a clue. It tells us that something in the system is out of alignment.

This section turns inward: how do we deal with our discomfort around inequality? Do we deny it? Justify it? Avoid it? Or do we sit with it—and let it change how we live?

Noticing Your Reaction

When you hear that Jeff Bezos added $13 billion to his net worth in one day, what happens in your body? Disgust? Envy? Disbelief? These aren't trivial feelings—they are data.

To grow in economic awareness, we must learn to feel without flinching. Discomfort is the first step to insight—and insight is the path to action.

Reflection Prompt 3: Where Does Inequality Make You Flinch?

Is it when you pass a beggar?

When you see a celebrity's closet tour on YouTube?

When you notice differences in your friend group?

Write about one moment when economic disparity shocked or unsettled you.

Transforming Discomfort Into Inquiry

Rather than suppress or weaponize discomfort, we can use it as a *tool for transformation*. Osnos encourages us not to blame, but to ask: What is this discomfort teaching me? What does it reveal about the world—and about myself?

Questions to ask:

- What do I assume about rich people?
- What do I fear about poverty?
- What am I avoiding by not talking about money?

Exercise: The Discomfort Journal

For one week, track your emotional reactions to money-related encounters:

- News headlines
- Shopping decisions
- Conversations about class

Rate each experience: + (positive), - (negative), or ~ (neutral).

At the end, review your patterns.

Choosing to See—Then Act

Ultimately, the cost of extreme wealth is *not seeing*. When yachts become normal, when suffering becomes invisible, when we ignore the ways we benefit from inequality—we become complicit.

But noticing is powerful. It opens the door to empathy, critique, and action. You don't need to fix everything—but you do need to *see clearly*. That is the first cost of wealth—and the first freedom of awareness.

"To feel discomfort in an unjust system is not failure—it is sanity."

Journal Prompt: What's One Thing You Can Do Differently?

Give more? Spend less? Talk honestly? Volunteer? Learn? Organize?

Start small—but start.

✅ Chapter 5 Summary:

- **Who Pays for the Yacht?** reveals that luxury depends on hidden labor, exploitation, and monopolized opportunity. Comfort is subsidized—often invisibly—by others' struggle.
- **The Emotional Toll of Inequality** exposes how both the ultra-rich and the economically excluded suffer in different ways: fear, shame, competition, and alienation.

- **Discomfort as a Compass** reminds us that noticing and naming inequality is the first act of resistance. When we lean into discomfort, we begin to see—and live—differently.

✍ ☐ Wrap-Up Reflection: The Cost You're Willing to Carry

Answer the following to conclude this chapter:

1. What's one hidden cost of your lifestyle that you've previously ignored?
2. How do you emotionally respond to other people's wealth—or poverty?
3. Where do you benefit from a system that disadvantages others?
4. What's one action—big or small—you can take to reduce the burden of inequality in your circle or society?

Chapter 6: Wealth Worship and Media Myths

Section 1: The Billionaire as Hero

From Forbes magazine covers to reality TV shows, billionaires are portrayed not just as rich—but as *geniuses*, *visionaries*, even *saviors*. They aren't just people with money. They are turned into modern demigods: faster, smarter, more efficient than the rest of us.

In *The Haves and the Have Yachts*, Evan Osnos peels back the curtain on this glorification and asks: What happens when we begin to *worship* wealth? What happens to a society that defines value by bank accounts and fame by net worth?

Myth #1: They're Smarter Than You

A common media narrative suggests that billionaires earned their status through intellect and innovation. Elon Musk, Jeff Bezos, Steve Jobs—these figures are portrayed as brilliant exceptions to the rule. But Osnos shows how many billionaires were born into privilege, relied on vast support systems, or simply capitalized on timing and deregulation.

Even when a rich person fails—think of a failed company or lawsuit—the narrative quickly shifts to resilience or reinvention. They aren't punished like ordinary people. They're applauded.

"In America, if a poor person fails, it's a tragedy. If a rich person fails, it's a startup."

Reflection Prompt 1: Who's the Smartest Person You Know?

Are they rich?

Why or why not?

How does society confuse intelligence with wealth?

Myth #2: They're the Job Creators

Another widespread belief is that billionaires are "job creators"—the engines of the economy. But Osnos points out the hypocrisy: many of the wealthiest individuals hoard profits, automate jobs, and lobby for policies that suppress worker power. Some outsource labor to exploit cheap markets while avoiding taxes in their home country.

Job creation is often a byproduct, not a mission. What drives the system is shareholder value, not social value.

Exercise: Track the Jobs

Pick a billionaire and research their business:

- How many jobs have they created?
- What do those jobs pay?
- Are workers unionized, protected, or disposable?

Myth #3: They Deserve It

This is perhaps the most powerful and dangerous myth—that billionaires deserve their wealth because they worked harder, took bigger risks, or added more value. This idea keeps ordinary people compliant. If billionaires *deserve* their status, then perhaps poverty is also deserved.

Osnos challenges this idea by highlighting how much billionaire success depends on **public goods**: government subsidies, public education, legal protections, and infrastructure. No billionaire builds alone.

Journal Prompt: How Do You Define 'Deserve'?

Who "deserves" comfort, education, opportunity?

Can someone "deserve" a billion dollars while others live without clean water?

Section 2: Media as a Mirror (and a Megaphone)

Media doesn't just reflect public values—it *shapes* them. Billionaires use magazines, streaming platforms, newspapers, and social media to craft their image. Osnos documents how the rich influence not just *what's said*, but *how it's said*—and what remains unsaid.

Controlling the Narrative

Many billionaires own media companies outright. Jeff Bezos owns *The Washington Post*. Elon Musk owns X (formerly Twitter). Others fund think tanks or pay for flattering documentaries and memoirs. This control ensures that their stories are told on *their* terms.

Criticism becomes rare, or at least softened. When the rich control the mic, dissent is edited out.

Reflection Prompt 2: Who Tells Your Story?

Who gets to tell your story—at work, in your community, or online?

Who tells the story of the wealthy? How often are they questioned?

The Lifestyle Fetish

Osnos also explores how media outlets like *Architectural Digest*, *Forbes*, *Bloomberg*, and Instagram glorify the *aesthetics* of wealth. From yacht tours to $10,000 watches to billionaire "morning routines," the audience is invited to *aspire*—not critique.

This constant exposure normalizes excess. When $500 million yachts become content, poverty becomes background noise.

Exercise: Audit Your Feed

Scroll through your Instagram, TikTok, or YouTube.

- How many luxury or wealth-themed posts do you see in 5 minutes?
- How do they make you feel—curious, jealous, numb, inspired?

Silencing the Ugly Truth

Stories about exploitation, inequality, or systemic injustice often receive less attention than celebrity gossip. Osnos emphasizes how media prioritizes stories that entertain, not educate.

Billionaires can commit environmental damage, suppress unions, or even influence elections—but these stories often vanish after one news cycle.

"Wealth doesn't just buy things—it buys silence."

Journal Prompt: What Story Deserves More Attention?

Is there a social issue, injustice, or community story that the media ignores?

Why do you think it gets overlooked?

Section 3: Rewriting the Narrative

If we want to dismantle wealth worship, we must become more conscious consumers of media. Osnos suggests that real change begins not only in policy, but in *perception*. The myths we buy are the myths we live by. It's time to tell better stories.

Humanizing, Not Idolizing

Instead of glorifying billionaires, we can start humanizing everyone. That means telling fuller, more complex stories:

- Stories of laborers and service workers
- Stories of communities fighting injustice
- Stories that celebrate resilience, not just riches

Osnos urges us to remember: a person's value is not their *net worth*, but their *human worth*.

Reflection Prompt 3: Whose Story Inspires You—and Why?

Is it a public figure? A family member? A historical leader?

What values does their story reflect that are *not* about money?

Creating Counter-Narratives

We can also push back by creating alternative narratives. This might mean:

- Supporting independent journalism
- Sharing stories that challenge consumerism
- Calling out inequality when it's glamorized

Change the story, and you change the culture.

Exercise: Your Personal Wealth Myth

Write down a message you absorbed growing up about wealth (e.g., "Rich people are happy," or "Money means safety.")

Now challenge it: Is it true? Where did it come from? What harm does it cause?

Choosing Your Aspirations

Ultimately, Osnos challenges us to rethink what we admire. Should we aspire to own more—or give more? Should we seek status—or significance? Our heroes reflect our hopes. If we want a better world, we need better role models.

"The opposite of wealth worship is not poverty glorification—it's *dignity for all*."

Journal Prompt: What Do You Aspire To?

Wealth? Freedom? Impact? Recognition?

How has your definition of success changed after reading this chapter?

✅ Chapter 6 Summary:

- **The Billionaire as Hero** reveals how myths of genius, job creation, and desert uphold inequality by turning wealth into virtue.

- **Media as a Mirror (and a Megaphone)** shows how billionaires control narratives and how media glamorizes wealth while silencing its darker sides.

- **Rewriting the Narrative** urges us to consume stories critically, uplift overlooked voices, and redefine what we admire.

✍ Wrap-Up Reflection: Media Detox and Myth Recovery

Take a moment to reflect deeply.

1. What are the top 3 wealth-related beliefs you've internalized from media?
2. How have these beliefs shaped your goals, values, or self-worth?
3. What's one media habit (TV show, podcast, account) you can cut or question?
4. What's one story—your own or someone else's—you want to tell more truthfully?

Chapter 7: Escaping the Yacht Trap – Reimagining Enough

Section 1: The Illusion of More

In *The Haves and the Have Yachts*, Evan Osnos gives us front-row seats to a world that spins endlessly toward more: bigger yachts, faster jets, more exclusive schools, higher property walls. This culture of escalation doesn't serve utility—it serves identity. But the truth Osnos reveals is quietly devastating: *more never satisfies*.

What keeps the wealth machine going isn't need. It's fear. Fear of being outdone, of falling behind, of becoming irrelevant even in wealth. And so the ultra-rich keep buying—not because they need, but because they *can't stop*. It's not abundance. It's addiction.

The Lifestyle Ratchet

Osnos introduces readers to billionaires whose first yachts "weren't enough." They were too small, too visible, too old. So they built new ones. But even then, someone else had something better. The cycle continues.

This is called the **lifestyle ratchet**—a psychological phenomenon where each gain becomes the new baseline. What was once a dream becomes normal. And what's normal becomes insufficient.

Reflection Prompt 1: Where Has Your "Enough" Shifted?

Think of something you once wanted deeply (a promotion, a car, a lifestyle).

Do you still appreciate it—or has your bar moved? Why?

Comparison as Currency

A key fuel in the trap is comparison. Osnos notes how billionaires compare everything: square footage, art collections, event invitations. It's less about joy and more about rank.

And it doesn't stop with the wealthy. We all do it. Social media, celebrity culture, and curated content feed us 24/7 comparisons. Someone always seems to have more: better vacations, newer tech, happier families.

This comparison economy ensures we never feel complete. If someone else has more, then what we have feels lacking—even when it's plenty.

Exercise: Envy Inventory

For one day, track every moment of financial or lifestyle envy (big or small).

Where did it come from? What did it trigger in you?

At the end, ask: Was that feeling rooted in desire—or comparison?

Scarcity in the Midst of Plenty

Ironically, those with the most often operate with a scarcity mindset. Osnos shows billionaires hoarding, hiding, and micromanaging wealth—not because they're greedy caricatures, but because they don't feel safe. More is always a shield—against irrelevance, against change, against truth.

This mindset bleeds into society. People who make six figures feel "behind." Corporations report record profits but still lay off workers. Entire industries exist to convince us that abundance means anxiety.

"If wealth brings security, why do the wealthiest seem the most afraid?"

Journal Prompt: What Does 'Enough' Mean to You Today?

Define "enough" in at least three areas: money, time, love, or recognition.

Be honest. What do you truly need to feel safe and fulfilled?

Section 2: Redefining Success and Status

To escape the trap of never-ending more, we need to challenge the very structures that define success and status. As Osnos suggests, the problem isn't just personal desire—it's cultural architecture. We must dismantle the symbols that define who matters and why.

The Tyranny of Metrics

Modern life is filled with metrics: salary, square footage, likes, followers, step counts, grades. While these numbers can offer structure, they also imprison us. They reduce complex human experiences into rankings. And they become addictive.

Billionaires are no exception. Osnos shows how their lives revolve around measurements—net worth, market influence, media attention. The pressure to *grow* never ends, even when they've already "won."

Reflection Prompt 2: What Do You Measure Most?

Time? Money? Productivity? Physical appearance?

How do those metrics shape your mood, your self-worth, your decisions?

Beyond the Resume

Part of the trap is professional. We often define ourselves by job titles, LinkedIn bios, or achievements. But Osnos introduces readers to billionaires who, despite their status, feel lost. They've built empires but lack connection. They've scaled heights but miss meaning.

What if success wasn't about climbing—but about contributing?

Exercise: Your Anti-Resume

Write a résumé of things that wouldn't go on a job application:

- Moments you made someone laugh
- Times you forgave someone
- Ways you made a space safer

These may not earn money—but they build legacy.

Status Without Superiority

Imagine a world where status wasn't based on money or possessions, but on generosity, wisdom, kindness, or creativity. Osnos points to rare individuals—some rich, some not—who have stepped out of the race.

These people refuse to compete. They redefine what matters. They value **enough** over **excess**. They recognize that when status depends on separation, it erodes community.

Journal Prompt: Who Do You Admire—And Why?

Is your admiration rooted in their wealth, fame, or something deeper?

What if your values shaped your heroes instead of the reverse?

Section 3: Cultivating a Life of Enough

If we are to resist the gravitational pull of the yacht trap, we must actively build an alternative. This doesn't mean rejecting ambition—but **redefining abundance**. Osnos leaves us with a challenge: Can we live lives that are full—not because they are *filled*, but because they are *grounded*?

Designing Your Enough

Enough is personal. For some, it's a quiet life. For others, it's community. For still others, it's the freedom to choose. The goal is not uniformity—it's clarity.

To find your enough, you need three things:

1. **Awareness** – notice where desire turns into distraction
2. **Honesty** – confront the stories you've inherited
3. **Discipline** – resist the default settings of consumer culture

Exercise: Enough Blueprint

Choose three areas of your life (e.g., home, work, spending, relationships).

For each, write down:

- What feels excessive
- What feels essential
- What you could let go of

Practicing Gratitude Without Complacency

Gratitude is not passivity. It's presence. It doesn't mean accepting injustice, but noticing what *already is*, not just what's missing.

Osnos notes how many people—rich or poor—live in constant hunger for the next thing. But gratitude reorients the soul. It brings balance.

Daily gratitude practice:

- Name three things you're grateful for (without qualifiers like "but…")
- Focus on *ordinary* things (a good sleep, a kind word, a moment of peace)

Journal Prompt: The Small Enoughs

Write a list titled "Today Was Enough Because…"

Fill it with small, specific moments of satisfaction.

Reclaiming Community and Interdependence

One reason billionaires build walls, yachts, and private islands is to escape *dependence*. Osnos shows how wealth isolates. But that isolation comes at a price: loneliness, distrust, surveillance.

What if enough meant **connection**, not control? What if the antidote to excessive wealth isn't minimalism—but **mutualism**?

Start local:

- Share tools with neighbors
- Join a local initiative or collective
- Offer time, not just money
- Value relationships as wealth

"The richest people in the world aren't those with the most—they're those who need the least to feel full."

✓ Chapter 7 Summary:

- **The Illusion of More** explains how comparison, scarcity thinking, and the lifestyle ratchet trap even the richest in an endless cycle of dissatisfaction.
- **Redefining Success and Status** encourages us to stop measuring worth by metrics and titles and start honoring generosity, humility, and community.
- **Cultivating a Life of Enough** offers practical steps to design a life rooted in clarity, connection, and meaning—not just accumulation.

Conclude this chapter with a 5-part reflection:

1. What area of your life feels driven by "more"? What would it take to stop?
2. Write your own definition of "enough" (in 1–2 sentences).
3. Who models "enoughness" in your life? How do they live?
4. What daily practice can help you reconnect with a sense of sufficiency?
5. Imagine a society where "enough" is celebrated instead of "more." What would change?

Chapter 8: Moving Toward Equity – Imagination and Action

Section 1: Naming the World We Want

To build a different world, we must first imagine it.

Evan Osnos's *The Haves and the Have Yachts* isn't just an exposé on wealth—it's a mirror, held up to an America obsessed with success, but unclear on value. The opulence of the ultra-rich—gleaming yachts, private islands, tax-free fortunes—isn't only a spectacle. It's a moral test. What kind of society makes this not only possible, but *normal*?

To confront this reality, we must ask: *What kind of world do we want instead?*

Beyond Envy, Beyond Shame

It's easy to feel stuck between emotions: envy of the rich and shame over our own privilege or lack. But these emotions, if not processed, keep us passive. They're tools of a status quo that thrives on confusion.

The first act of liberation is clarity. As Osnos makes clear: we must move from being spectators of inequality to **designers of equity**.

"A better world won't emerge from disgust alone. It will grow from imagination."

Reflection Prompt 1: Picture the World You Want

Close your eyes and picture your ideal community.

What does safety look like? What does fairness feel like?

How are resources shared? How is dignity protected?

Justice is Not Just Fairness—It's Repair

Equity doesn't mean giving everyone the same. It means correcting for harm, history, and hoarded advantage. Osnos invites readers to think not only in terms of *equality* but *restoration*— repairing systems that have long favored the few over the many.

Justice means:

- Affordable housing and healthcare
- Living wages and dignified work
- Fair taxation and transparent governance
- The dismantling of systemic racism, classism, and exclusion

These aren't fantasies. They're overdue promises.

Exercise: Map the Gaps

Pick one system: education, healthcare, transportation, housing, or finance.

List:

- Who benefits most?
- Who is left behind?
- What change would close the gap?

Vision Requires Vocabulary

We can't build what we can't name. That's why new language matters. We need words beyond "billionaire," "charity," or "success." We need shared terms for:

- **Dignity without wealth**
- **Community without consumption**
- **Security without hoarding**

Osnos helps us see: new systems require new stories—and new stories require new words.

Journal Prompt: Define Your Values

Write your own definitions for five words:

- Enough
- Power
- Community
- Responsibility
- Justice

Section 2: Living Differently in a Broken System

Osnos doesn't call for perfection—but for consciousness. We can't immediately fix billionaires, lobbying, or tax loopholes. But we *can* live differently in the meantime. We can choose lives that reflect the future we want.

Personal Practice as Political Power

The way we spend, consume, vote, and connect *matters*. When multiplied across communities, these habits shape culture. Culture shapes policy. Policy shapes systems.

Some practices to consider:

- **Spending mindfully**: Who profits from your purchases?
- **Giving with accountability**: Who sets the terms—donor or community?
- **Voting with knowledge**: Who funds the candidates you support?
- **Working with purpose**: How does your labor feed the system?

Exercise: Your Power Audit

Create a table with these categories:

- Time
- Money
- Skills
- Influence

List:

1. Where you currently invest them
2. Where you *want* to invest them to support equity

Wealth Isn't Just Money—It's Orientation

We often define wealth narrowly—money, assets, security. But Osnos's reporting shows how shallow this becomes when disconnected from meaning. The richest people in the book are often also the most afraid.

So what if wealth wasn't accumulation, but **contribution**?

True wealth includes:

- The ability to help without fear
- The freedom to rest
- The joy of shared belonging
- The presence of purpose

Reflection Prompt 2: Your Wealth, Redefined

List 10 ways you are already "wealthy" that have nothing to do with money.

Which of these would you share freely if society truly rewarded generosity?

Rejecting the Savior Complex

It's tempting to think *we* can fix the world. But as Osnos emphasizes, wealthy philanthropy often perpetuates the very systems it claims to address. Real change doesn't come from saviors. It comes from **solidarity**.

Instead of:

- "How can I help?" → ask: **"Who is already leading, and how can I follow?"**
- "What can I give?" → ask: **"What would it mean to give up control?"**
- "What should be done?" → ask: **"Who is directly affected, and what do they say they need?"**

Journal Prompt: Whose Voices Do You Listen To?

In your work, news, and circles—who do you hear most?

Who's missing? Who's silenced? What might change if you made space?

Section 3: Collective Action and Long-Term Change

Change doesn't happen alone. Osnos shows us that the structures enabling extreme wealth were built collectively—and they must be *unbuilt* collectively too.

From Awareness to Organizing

Awareness is the spark, but action is the flame. Osnos doesn't leave us in abstraction. He points to organizers, reformers, and regular citizens who demand accountability, organize unions, reform tax codes, and build alternatives.

Some examples of real-world equity work:

- **Policy reform** (wealth taxes, campaign finance laws, universal basic income)
- **Worker organizing** (Amazon, Starbucks, gig economy)
- **Community wealth building** (credit unions, land trusts, food co-ops)
- **Civic education** (learning how power actually works—then disrupting it)

Exercise: Pick Your Entry Point

Of the examples above, which excites or angers you most?

Do a 10-minute web search. Find:

- A group doing that work near you
- A newsletter, local action, or upcoming event

You don't have to be an expert—just willing to learn.

Civic Courage in an Unjust Economy

Courage is choosing truth in a world that rewards silence. It means:

- Speaking up about injustice at work, school, or church
- Asking uncomfortable questions in safe spaces
- Staying in hard conversations
- Resisting the urge to check out

Osnos shows us that civic courage isn't rare—it's buried. Under fatigue, under fear, under distraction. But it's there, waiting.

"The opposite of comfort is not hardship—it's consciousness."

Reflection Prompt 3: What's Your Civic Risk Tolerance?

What's the boldest justice-oriented action you've ever taken?

What stopped you from doing more?

What would it take to take one more step?

Imagination as Resistance

Finally, change begins with **imagination**. The billionaires Osnos profiles have yachts built to escape climate collapse, social unrest, even revolution. They are planning for survival—not solidarity.

Let's imagine something better.

Imagine:

- A tax system where loopholes are closed and funds are reinvested in schools
- A public health system that prioritizes prevention, not profit
- A housing system where stability isn't for sale

- A media system where truth outweighs celebrity

- A justice system rooted in repair, not revenge

None of these are fantasy. They are possible—if enough people *refuse to stop imagining*.

Journal Prompt: The World After the Yacht

Describe a day in a world where extreme wealth has been redistributed, and dignity has been democratized.

How do you wake up? Who do you talk to? What feels different in your body?

✅ Chapter 8 Summary:

- **Naming the World We Want** challenges us to define justice in positive terms—not just what we oppose, but what we build.
- **Living Differently in a Broken System** reminds us that our values are expressed through action, not perfection.
- **Collective Action and Long-Term Change** affirms that the path forward is shared, political, and powered by imagination and solidarity.

✍️ Wrap-Up Reflection: What Now?

Conclude your journey through this workbook with these final prompts:

1. What was your biggest mindset shift while reading *The Haves and the Have Yachts* and this workbook?
2. What myths about wealth or success have you now released?
3. What specific action will you take in the next 30 days to support equity—at home, in work, or in public life?

4. What long-term dream will you now dare to imagine, not because it's easy, but because it's *necessary*?

👣 Final Note: You Are Not Powerless

If billionaires have shown us anything, it's that systems respond to influence. But power doesn't belong to them alone. It belongs to us—when we claim it together, when we tell better stories, when we live in alignment with what we know to be right.

You are not alone.

You are not too late.

You are not without tools.

You've finished the workbook—but the work continues.

☐ BONUS TOOLKIT: Moving from Reflection to Action

✅ Practical Actions for Equity-Minded Living

1. Spend With Purpose

- Choose small/local over corporate when possible.
- Use "ethical consumer" tools like Good On You or DoneGood.
- Ask: *Who profits? Who pays?*

2. Share Power

- Hire inclusively, mentor generously, speak up in rooms others aren't in.
- Give credit, step back, listen more than you lead.

3. Give with Impact

- Support community-based mutual aid, not just top-down charities.
- Give recurring donations, not just one-offs.

4. Educate Yourself

- Subscribe to newsletters from marginalized voices.
- Attend equity trainings, policy discussions, or city forums.

5. Advocate and Organize

- Call representatives about tax reform, education funding, or housing justice.
- Join local coalitions, book clubs, or advocacy groups.

📖 FURTHER READING: Books to Expand Your Lens

On Wealth and Inequality:

- *Winners Take All* – Anand Giridhara Das

- *Capital in the Twenty-First Century* – Thomas Piketty
- *The Sum of Us* – Heather McGhee
- *Nickel and Dimed* – Barbara Ehrenreich
- *The Divide* – Matt Taibbi

On Power, Philanthropy, and Reform:

- *Decolonizing Wealth* – Edgar Villanueva
- *Just Giving* – Rob Reich
- *Mutual Aid* – Dean Spade
- *From What Is to What If* – Rob Hopkins

On Vision, Imagination, and Justice:

- *Emergent Strategy* – adrienne maree brown
- *Utopia for Realists* – Rutger Bregman
- *Pleasure Activism* – adrienne maree brown
- *Hope in the Dark* – Rebecca Solnit

GUIDED JOURNAL: 10 Prompts to Deepen the Journey

Use one each day—or revisit when you need grounding.

1. **What does enough feel like in your body?** Describe the sensation.
2. **Where are you complicit in systems you oppose?** What one change can you make?
3. **What stories about rich people shaped your youth?** Are they still influencing you?

4. **Who taught you about dignity?** How do they live?

5. **What would you do if status didn't matter at all?**

6. **What would it mean to be rich in time, not money?**

7. **Who do you owe solidarity to—not charity, but shared struggle?**

8. **What one privilege could you redistribute today?**

9. **If justice were a room, what would it look like? Who would be inside?**

10. **What does "a good life" mean to you now?** How is it different than before?

✆ Closing Invocation: Living Awake

"We cannot unsee what we have seen.

We cannot unknow what we have learned.

We are not meant to live numb—but live true.

Let every dollar be a question. Let every choice be a chance.

Let this workbook not be an end—but a door."

Made in United States
Orlando, FL
22 July 2025

63158126R00039